# THE 64 KALAS OF KRISHNA FOR SCHOOL CHILDREN

DR DHEERAJ MEHROTRA

# Contents

# Preface

*The leadership skills of Lord Krishna are a benchmark with so much learning and practical applications in our lives. The book "The 64 Kalas of Lord Krishna for School Children" is a broader step to promote the skills needed for our kids to face the future with delight,*

*confidence and commitment.*

*As we all celebrate the auspicious festival of Krisha Janamasthmi every year, it is high time to assess how many of Krisha's 64-Kalas are relevant and beneficial for our students and how many are promoted in our schools as a priority.*

*Best*

*Author*

*www.authordheerajmehrotra.com*

# CHAPTER ONE

# 64 Kalas of Krishna For School Children

*1. Singing:*

*Music instruction expects students to perceive and rehash words' pitch, tone or articulation. Particularly in small kids, music straightforwardly helps the capacity to learn words, talk them accurately, and process the many new sounds they hear from others. Music instruction includes a high degree of remembrance.*

*Singing is a valuable activity for children as it provides many benefits that can positively impact their development and well-being. Here are some reasons why singing is essential in the lives of kids:*

*Language Development: Singing helps children develop their language skills by improving their vocabulary, sentence structure, and phonemic awareness. It also helps them learn how to communicate through music, an essential life skill.*

*Cognitive Development: Singing has been shown to improve children's memory, attention, and overall cognitive functioning. It helps them learn how to focus, process information, and think creatively.*

*Emotional Expression: Singing allows children to express themselves emotionally, safely and constructively. It can help them manage their emotions, reduce stress and anxiety, and develop healthy coping mechanisms.*

*Social Skills: Singing in groups helps children develop social skills such as cooperation, teamwork, and communication. It provides opportunities for children to connect with others and build friendships.*

*Confidence and Self-Esteem: Singing helps children build confidence and self-esteem as they learn to use their voices and express themselves in front of others. It can help them feel more comfortable and confident in social situations and public speaking.*

*Cultural Awareness: Singing exposes children to different musical styles and cultures, helping them appreciate and understand diversity. It also helps them learn about other traditions and customs worldwide.*

*2. Instrumental music:*

*Instrumental music projects can empower students to develop scholastically while fostering their fine engine control and social capacities to make them functioning, mindful citizens. Instrumental music can alike empower kids to encounter the inventive approach.*

*Instrumental music is a valuable activity for children as it provides numerous benefits that can positively impact their development and well-being. Here are some reasons why instrumental music is essential in the lives of kids:*

*Cognitive Development: Playing an instrument involves many cognitive processes, such as memory, attention, and problem-solving. This helps children improve their cognitive abilities and academic performance.*

*Emotional Expression: Playing an instrument allows children to express themselves emotionally, safely and constructively. It can help them manage their emotions, reduce stress and anxiety, and develop healthy coping mechanisms.*

*Motor Skills: Playing an instrument involves physical movement and coordination, which can help children develop their fine motor skills and hand-eye coordination.*

*Discipline and Focus: Learning to play an instrument requires discipline and focus, as it involves consistent practice and attention to detail. This can help children develop these* essential life skills that can benefit them in other areas.

Social Skills: Playing an instrument can provide opportunities for children to connect with others and build friendships. It also helps them develop essential social skills such as cooperation, teamwork, and communication.

Cultural Awareness: Playing an instrument exposes children to different musical styles and cultures, helping them appreciate and understand diversity. It also helps them learn about other traditions and customs worldwide.

3. Dancing:

'Dance is significant in schools because it allows us to inspire and motivate others to come off their shell and express themselves through movement, emotion and music. It also brings everyone together, as we are all equal and share the same ambition and dreams.

Dancing is an essential activity for school kids as it provides numerous benefits that can *positively impact their physical, emotional, and social well-being. Here are some reasons why dancing is essential in the lives of school kids:*

*Physical Fitness: Dancing is a great way to exercise and improve physical fitness. It can help kids develop endurance, strength, flexibility, and coordination.*

*Emotional Expression: Dancing allows kids to express themselves emotionally, safely and constructively. It can help them manage their emotions, reduce stress and anxiety, and develop healthy coping mechanisms.*

*Self-Confidence: Dancing can help kids build self-confidence as they learn to move their bodies and express themselves in front of others. It can also help them feel more comfortable and confident in social situations and public speaking.*

*Social Skills: Dancing can provide opportunities for kids to connect with others and build friendships. It also helps them develop essential social skills such as cooperation, teamwork, and communication.*

*Cultural Awareness: Dancing exposes kids to different dance styles worldwide, helping them appreciate and understand diversity. It also helps them learn about other cultures' different traditions and customs.*

*Creativity: Dancing allows kids to explore their creativity and imagination. It can help them develop their artistic skills and encourage them to think outside the box.*

*4. Painting:*

*It improves motor skills; simple things like mastering a paintbrush or using crayons and pencils help develop more refined motor skills, especially in younger children.*

*Dancing is an essential activity for school kids as it provides numerous benefits that can positively impact their physical, emotional, and social well-being. Here are some reasons why dancing is essential in the lives of school kids:*

*Physical Fitness: Dancing is a great way to exercise and improve physical fitness. It can help kids develop endurance, strength, flexibility, and coordination.*

*Emotional Expression: Dancing allows kids to express themselves emotionally, safely and constructively. It can help them manage their emotions, reduce stress and anxiety, and develop healthy coping mechanisms.*

*Self-Confidence: Dancing can help kids build self-confidence as they learn to move their bodies and express themselves in front of others. It can also help them feel more comfortable and confident in social situations and public speaking.*

*Social Skills: Dancing can provide opportunities for kids to connect with others and build friendships. It also helps them develop essential social skills such as cooperation, teamwork, and communication.*

*Cultural Awareness: Dancing exposes kids to different dance styles worldwide, helping them* appreciate and understand diversity. It also helps them learn about other cultures' different traditions and customs.

Creativity: Dancing allows kids to explore their creativity and imagination. It can help them develop their artistic skills and encourage them to think outside the box.

5. Forehead Adornments:

A unique feature of Krishna can help develop the skill of TILAK on the forehead symbolising a relaxed mind and preparedness for the day of learning.

Forehead adornments, also known as "bindis," are an everyday decorative accessory worn by women in South Asian cultures. These adornments have cultural and religious significance and are special in many people's lives. Here are some of the relevance and importance of forehead adornments in life:

*Cultural and Religious Significance: Forehead adornments have a significant cultural and religious significance in many South Asian cultures. They are worn as a symbol of spirituality, purity, and devotion.*

*Aesthetics: Forehead adornments add an aesthetic element to an outfit, often adding a pop of colour or sparkle. They can be worn as a fashion statement or to enhance a company.*

*Personal Expression: Forehead adornments can also be a form of personal expression. They can express one's personality, style, or mood.*

*Tradition and Heritage: Wearing forehead adornments can be a way to honour and preserve one's cultural heritage and traditions.*

*Spiritual and Emotional Well-Being: For some people, wearing forehead adornments can have a spiritual or emotional significance. It can provide comfort and connection to one's beliefs and spirituality.*

6. *Making decorative floral and grain designs on the floor:*

*We may refer to it as art on the floor. It may symbolize a flower decoration on the floor made during Onam celebrations in Kerala. Also known as pookalam in Malayalam.*

*Making decorative floral and grain designs on the floor, also known as "Rangoli" or "Kolam," is a traditional art form that originated in India. It is integral to many cultural and religious celebrations and holds a special place in many people's lives. Here are some reasons why making decorative floral and grain designs on the floor is essential:*

*Cultural Significance: Making decorative floral and grain designs on the floor is an essential cultural tradition in many parts of India. It is integral to festivals and celebrations and reflects the country's rich cultural heritage.*

*Aesthetic Value: Making these designs is an art form that adds beauty and aesthetic value to the surroundings. It creates a vibrant and festive atmosphere, and it can be a way to express creativity and artistic skills.*

*Religious Significance: Making decorative floral and grain designs on the floor is integral to religious rituals and ceremonies in many*

Indian traditions. It is believed to bring good luck, prosperity, and blessings to the home and the family.

Community Building: Making these designs can be communal, bringing people together to create something beautiful and meaningful. It can promote a sense of community and belonging.

Mindfulness and Relaxation: Making decorative floral and grain designs on the floor can also be meditative and relaxing. It requires focus and attention to detail and can help reduce stress and anxiety.

7. Home and temple flower arranging: Well, an art of perfection. In addition to beautifying our surroundings, flower arranging encourages improved manual dexterity promotes sensory stimulation and reduces stress.

Home and temple flower arranging is an art form that involves the skilful arrangement of flowers and other natural materials into beautiful and aesthetically pleasing designs. This art form has cultural, spiritual, and *aesthetic significance in many parts of the world, including South Asian and East Asian cultures. Here are some reasons why home and temple flower arranging is essential in our lives:*

*Aesthetic Value: Home and temple flower arranging add aesthetic value to our surroundings. It creates beautiful and visually appealing designs that can enhance the beauty of a space.*

*Spiritual Significance: In many cultures, home and temple flower arranging is considered a sacred art form with spiritual significance. It is often used as an offering to deities or to honour ancestors.*

*Cultural Significance: Home and temple flower arranging is essential to many cultural traditions and celebrations. It reflects the cultural heritage of a community and helps preserve cultural identity.*

*Environmental Awareness: Home and temple flower arranging encourages an appreciation for nature and promotes environmental awareness. It involves using natural materials and encourages the conservation of natural resources.*

*Personal Expression: Home and temple flower arranging can also be private. It allows individuals to showcase their creativity and artistic skills and express their unique perspectives and tastes.*

*Mindfulness and Relaxation: Home and temple flower arranging can also be meditative and relaxing. It requires focus and attention to detail and can help reduce stress and anxiety.*

*8. Personal grooming: This requires grooming our personality to the attire and upkeep for our kids. The priority should be to also Keep school bags clean and free from food remnants, especially if your child carries a packed lunch to school. Gym clothes should be brought home once a week for washing. Make sure your children change their socks and underwear daily. Wash school uniforms at a high temperature to kill bacteria.*

Personal grooming refers to individuals' practices and routines to maintain their physical appearance and hygiene. It involves bathing, brushing teeth, hair care, skin care, and dressing appropriately. Personal grooming is essential in our lives for the following reasons:

Health and Hygiene: Personal grooming is essential for maintaining good health and hygiene. Regular bathing, brushing teeth, and other grooming practices help prevent the spread of germs and reduce the risk of infections and diseases.

Professional and Social Success: A well-groomed appearance can help individuals make an excellent first impression in professional and social settings. It can increase confidence and self-esteem and improve opportunities for success.

Self-Care and Wellness: Personal grooming can be a form of self-care and wellness. It allows individuals to take time, prioritise their needs, and practice self-love.

Cultural and Social Norms: Personal grooming is expected and considered a sign of respect *and proper etiquette in many cultures and social settings. Failing to meet these expectations can lead to social ostracization and negative judgments.*

*Mental Health: Personal grooming can also positively impact mental health. It can help individuals feel more confident, improve mood and self-esteem, and reduce stress and anxiety.*

*9. Mosaic tiling: Children learn about shapes and how they fit together through mosaic art. They are introduced to patterns and can practice fine motor skills while using their imagination and decision-making skills.*

*Mosaic tiling is an art form that involves creating pictures or patterns by arranging small pieces of coloured glass, stone, or other materials. It is a creative and engaging activity that can be a great hobby or skill for kids to learn in schools. Here are some reasons why mosaic tiling can be an excellent activity for kids:*

*Creative Expression: Mosaic tiling allows kids to express their creativity and imagination by* creating unique designs and patterns. It provides a platform for kids to showcase their artistic talents and develop their unique style.

*Fine Motor Skills:* Mosaic tiling requires fine motor skills such as hand-eye coordination, precision, and agility. Engaging in mosaic tiling can help develop these skills in kids, which can be helpful in other areas of their lives.

*Patience and Persistence:* Mosaic tiling is a time-consuming process that requires patience and persistence. Kids who engage in mosaic tiling learn to work through challenges and setbacks, develop perseverance, and understand the value of hard work and dedication.

*Cultural and Historical Significance:* Mosaic tiling has a rich cultural and historical significance. It has been used in art and architecture for thousands of years and is integral to many cultural traditions. By learning about the history and cultural importance of mosaic tiling, kids can develop a deeper appreciation for art and culture.

*Collaborative Learning: Mosaic tiling can be a great cooperative learning activity. Kids can work together to create large-scale projects and learn to communicate and work effectively in a team.*

*10. Bedroom arrangements: The kids are always excited about their rooms, and A simple string of fairy lights is a great way of adding a warm glow to a child's room or illuminating a dark corner.*

*Bedroom arrangements for kids are an essential consideration for parents to ensure that their children have a comfortable and safe environment to sleep and play in. Here are some key factors to consider when arranging a bedroom for kids:*

*Safety: The priority when arranging a bedroom for kids is to ensure it is safe. This includes checking that furniture and decor are securely anchored to the walls to prevent tipping and ensuring that cords and electrical outlets are out of reach.*

*Sleeping Space: It's essential to ensure the child's bed is safe and comfortable, away from hazards such as windows or sharp edges. The mattress should be relaxed, and the bedding should be age-appropriate and conducive to a good night's sleep.*

*Storage: Storage is essential in a child's bedroom to help keep the space organized and clutter-free. This can include bookshelves, toy bins, and dressers, and it should be easily accessible for the child to use independently.*

*Play Space: Providing a designated play space in the child's bedroom is essential to encourage imagination and creativity. This can include a play tent, a small table for arts and crafts, or a cosy reading nook.*

*Personalization: Kids often enjoy having a say in their bedroom decor. Let them choose colours, artwork, and decor items they love, as this can help foster a sense of ownership and pride in their space.*

*Lighting: Proper lighting is essential for a child's bedroom to ensure it is safe and conducive to sleep. This can include a combination of overhead lighting and bedside lamps for reading.*

*11. Creating music with water: This is an excellent science in practice. Tapping the spoon on the glass creates a vibration sending a sound*

*wave through the water in the mirror. Each glass makes a different sound because the sound wave travels at different speeds through the water. The rate of the sound wave depends on the amount of water in the glass.*

*Creating music with water is a fun and educational activity for kids that can help develop their creativity, motor skills, and musical abilities. Here are some tips for teaching kids how to create music with water:*

*Start with simple materials: You only need a few glasses or jars of varying sizes, water, and a spoon. You can add food colouring to the water to make it more visually appealing.*

*Teach the basics: Start by teaching kids how to create different sounds by tapping the glasses with the spoon. Explain how the size and amount of water in each glass affect the sound that it produces.*

*Experiment with pitches: Encourage kids to experiment with different angles by filling the glasses with varying amounts of water. You can also have them try tapping the glasses with different types of objects, such as pencils or chopsticks, to create different sounds.*

*Add melodies: Once kids have mastered the basics, challenge them to create songs by tapping notes on the glasses. You can also encourage them to sing or hum along to the melody as they play.*

*Incorporate other instruments: To take the activity to the next level, you can encourage kids to incorporate other devices, such as a keyboard or guitar, to play with the water music.*

*12. Splashing and squirting with water: This is an art in practice. Children work on their fine motor skills by squirting, pouring, and stirring the water.*

*Splashing and squirting with water is a fun and engaging activity that provides kids with physical and sensory benefits. Here are some of the benefits of splashing and spraying with water for kids:*

*Gross motor development: Splashing and squirting with water can help develop gross motor skills as kids engage in physical movements such as bending, reaching, and twisting. These movements can help improve balance, coordination, and overall strength.*

*Sensory development: Splashing and squirting with water can also provide sensory input, which can help with sensory processing and regulation. The sensation of water on the skin can be calming and soothing for some kids while providing an opportunity for exploration and experimentation.*

*Creative expression: Splashing and squirting with water can be fun for kids to express their creativity and imagination. They can experiment with different splashing and spraying methods, such as creating patterns or trying to hit targets.*

*Social skills: Splashing and squirting with water can also be an excellent way for kids to interact with others and develop social skills. It provides an opportunity for cooperative play and can encourage communication and teamwork.*

*A safe and supervised environment is essential when splashing and squirting with water. Kids should always be supervised while playing with water. Appropriate safety measures should be taken, such as ensuring that the area is free from hazards and that kids wear proper clothing and footwear.*

*13. Secret mantras: We start in the school with the chanting of OM. Mantras for children are words, sounds, statements or slogans repeated frequently to attune with intentional energy or quality. Mantra soothes the mind and increases attention span. It creates self-confidence in children to serve and act cheerfully in their immediate surroundings, and it helps them nurture their creativity.*

*The concept of secret mantras for kids can be interpreted in different ways. Here are a few possibilities:*

*Positive affirmations: You can teach your kids positive affirmations or mantras to repeat to themselves to promote self-confidence and self-esteem. These mantras can be simple phrases such as "I am strong," "I am capable," or "I can do anything I set my mind to." By repeating these mantras, kids can train their minds to focus on positive thoughts and beliefs about themselves.*

*Mindfulness techniques: Another form of secret mantra for kids could be mindfulness techniques such as deep breathing or visualization exercises. You can teach your kids to take a few deep breaths and repeat a calming mantra or visualization when they feel stressed or overwhelmed. This can help them regulate their emotions and stay grounded in the present moment.*

*Personal values: You can also help your kids identify and cultivate their values or mantras, such as kindness, honesty, or perseverance. By encouraging them to reflect on their values and to live in alignment with them, you can help them develop a sense of purpose and direction in life.*

*The key to introducing secret mantras to kids is to make them age-appropriate and engaging. You can make it into a game, use fun visuals or drawings, or make it a daily ritual. The goal is to help kids develop a positive mindset, emotional resilience, and inner strength to support them throughout their lives.*

*14. Making flower garlands: Like many other classical art forms, Garland stringing is also reported to be very meditative and therapeutic. It enhances mental focus and concentration and fuels creativity and imagination, thus becoming an excellent exercise for the brain and mind. Many doctors and psychiatrists today declare that besides being a good stress buster, this skill has proved to be very helpful for kids and adults with disabilities like dyslexia, anxiety, depression and other mental illness.*

*15. Head adornments: An adornment is generally an accessory or ornament worn to enhance the beauty or status of the wearer. For wearing on the Head, they are termed as Head Adornments.*

*16. Dressing: Dressing oneself comprises choosing articles of clothing and footwear, putting them on, securing them using various types of fasteners, and removing them.*

*17. Costume decorations: Putting on a costume is a creative play. Research has shown that participating in imaginative play may enhance a person's problem-solving skills and capacity to exercise self-control. Children conceive a variety of situations and places, as well as different social behaviours, and then act them out via play. They can try new ways of thinking and acting without affecting their regular habits, which is a huge benefit. Children's ability to communicate with others and think creatively may both benefit from time spent playing dress-up.*

*18. Perfumery, It is possible for a perfumer to communicate intangible ideas and states of* mind via the aroma compositions of perfume. A perfumer must have a deep understanding of a wide range of fragrance compounds and how they smell, as well as the ability to differentiate between the smells of each fragrance ingredient regardless of whether it is used alone or in conjunction with other scents. A perfumer can communicate intangible ideas and states of mind via the aroma compositions of perfume.

19. *Jewellery-making Crafts for Children Appropriate for Preschoolers Include Jewelry. Creating Straw beads, pony beads, and even metallic-painted pasta are excellent materials for children of preschool age to use when making jewellery. You may also get started with clay jewellery made with cookie cutters or other elementary methods to do with clay.*

*20. Magic and illusions, magic involves executing tricks to make the seemingly impossible seem achievable. Magicians can astonish audiences by creating the illusion that they can do things such as make items vanish, read minds, or float off the ground.*

*21. Skincare, especially protection from sunburn, is essential for students in schools for several reasons:*

*Health: Exposure to the sun's harmful ultraviolet (UV) rays can cause skin damage, premature ageing, and even skin cancer. Students can reduce their risk of developing these conditions by protecting their skin from sunburn.*

*Comfort: Sunburn can be painful and uncomfortable, making it difficult for students to focus and learn in school. Students can avoid this discomfort and stay comfortable throughout the school day by taking steps to prevent sunburn.*

*Safety: Sunburn can also increase the risk of heat stroke and dehydration, especially during the hot summer. Students can stay safe and healthy while attending school by protecting their skin from sunburn.*

*Education: By teaching students about the importance of sun protection and skin care, schools can help them develop healthy habits they can carry with them throughout their lives.*

*This can also help students become more informed and responsible regarding their health and wellness.*

22. *Manual dexterity, The ability to manage items with your hands in a deft, coordinated manner while making tiny, exact motions is known as manual dexterity. Manual dexterity is the ability to use your hands and fingers skillfully to perform tasks that require precision and coordination. It is an important skill to teach in schools for several reasons:*

*Manual dexterity is critical for developing fine motor skills. Fine motor skills are essential for writing, typing, playing musical instruments, and manipulating small objects.*

*Manual skill is essential for completing daily activities, such as tying shoelaces, buttoning clothes, and using cutlery. Developing manual talent in schools can help students become more independent in their everyday life.*

*Manual dexterity is also essential for safety reasons. For example, safely handling and manipulating tools and equipment requires good manual skills.*

*Many jobs require good manual skills, like healthcare, dentistry, mechanics, and construction. Teaching manual dexterity skills in schools can prepare students for future career paths.*

*Manual dexterity is also essential for artistic pursuits such as drawing, painting, and sculpting. Developing good manual dexterity can help students express themselves creatively.*

*Developing good manual dexterity can boost confidence and self-esteem. Students who can quickly complete tasks that require manual dexterity are more likely to feel confident and capable in other areas of their lives.*

*23. Skills in cooking, eating and drinking: Cooking is a valuable life skill often linked with improved diet quality, such as enhancing fruit and vegetable uptake and increasing recognition of healthier foods. Developing cooking, eating, and drinking skills can be essential for school students. Here are some key reasons why:*

*Promotes healthy habits: Learning to cook healthy meals and make healthy food choices can encourage students to adopt healthy habits that can last a lifetime. Students who learn about proper nutrition and meal planning can be better equipped to make informed decisions about what they eat and drink.*

*Teaches life skills: Cooking, eating, and drinking are essential life skills that students will need as they grow up and become more independent. Students can gain confidence and self-sufficiency by learning these skills in school.*

*Enhances cultural understanding: Food is an essential part of many cultures. Learning about different cuisines and cooking techniques can help students develop a deeper understanding and appreciation for other cultures.*

*Fosters creativity: Cooking can be a creative process that encourages experimentation and innovation. Students can learn to express themselves through food and develop their creativity by creating their culinary skills.*

*Provides career opportunities: The food industry is a significant employer, and students who develop skills in cooking, eating, and drinking can explore career opportunities in this field. These skills can be precious for students pursuing culinary arts or hospitality careers.*

*24. Beverage and dessert preparation, A priority towards cooking well. Knowing how to prepare beverages and desserts is a valuable life skill that students can use throughout their lives. They can apply this knowledge to entertain friends and family and to make healthier choices by avoiding pre-packaged and processed options.*

*Preparing beverages and desserts in school can also help students understand the nutritional value of different ingredients and encourage them to choose healthier options. Students can make informed decisions about what they consume by understanding the nutritional content of other beverages and desserts.*

*Beverage and dessert preparation allows students to express their creativity by experimenting with different flavours and ingredients. They can also learn how to decorate desserts artistically and appealingly.*

*Preparing beverages and desserts involves measuring and combining ingredients, which provides a hands-on opportunity for students to learn and apply math and science concepts.*

*Beverages and desserts are often deeply tied to cultural traditions and celebrations. Students can better understand and appreciate other cultures by learning about different artistic drinks and desserts.*

*Students can also learn entrepreneurship skills by developing their beverage and dessert recipes and selling them at school events or community markets.*

*25. Sewing(making and mending garments) is an art which can be taught to children as a part of life skills. Sewing is a practical life skill that students can use throughout their lives. Sewing and mending clothing can save money and extend the life of garments, which is particularly important in a world where sustainability and resource conservation are becoming increasingly important.*

*Sewing is also a creative outlet that allows students to express themselves through fashion and design. It allows students to customize their clothing and create unique garments that reflect their style and taste. Sewing requires fine motor skills, crucial for various activities, such as writing, typing, and playing musical instruments. By practising sewing, students can improve their hand-eye coordination and agility, which can translate to other areas of their lives. Sewing requires critical thinking and problem-solving skills. Students must understand patterns and measurements, identify mistakes, and troubleshoot problems that arise during the sewing process.*

*And finally, Sewing has a rich cultural history, and learning how to sew can help students appreciate the role that clothing plays in different cultures. Students can learn about traditional clothing and styles from various regions and periods, which can deepen their understanding of history and culture.*

26. *Embroidery is again an art which can be taught to kids in schools. Embroidery allows students to express their creativity and individuality through art. This can be especially beneficial for students who may not excel in traditional academic subjects but find joy in artistic pursuits.*

*Embroidery requires precise hand movements and talent, which can help students develop fine motor skills. This can be particularly useful for younger students still developing their motor skills.*

*Embroidery has a long history and is found in many different cultures worldwide. By teaching embroidery in schools, students can learn about this art form's cultural and historical context and gain a deeper appreciation for its significance.*

*Embroidery can be a slow and meticulous process, requiring patience and perseverance. Teaching students this skill can help them learn the value of persistence and hard work, which can translate to other areas of their lives.*

*27. Playing vena and drums has always been a pride for kids. This may be encouraged in schools at all levels. Playing musical instruments such as vena and drums can benefit students, making them an essential part of school curriculums. Here are some of the critical reasons why playing veena and drums in schools is essential:*

*Enhances creativity: Music can spark creativity and encourage students to think outside the box. Playing veena and drums can help students develop musical creativity and explore new ideas.*

*Develops coordination: Playing musical instruments requires high hand-eye coordination, which can benefit students' overall development.*

*Improves concentration: Playing veena and drums requires a high level of focus and attention, which can help students improve their concentration and attention spans.*

*Boosts confidence: Mastering a musical instrument can give students a sense of accomplishment and boost their confidence, positively impacting their overall well-being.*

*Encourages teamwork: Playing in a musical ensemble requires collaboration and teamwork, which can help students develop critical social skills and learn to work with others.*

*Enhances cultural appreciation: Playing traditional Indian instruments like veena can help students better appreciate their cultural heritage and the rich history of Indian classical music.*

*28. Riddles and rhymes have been a priority for the nursery and primary children and should be an art to teach as a priority. Riddles and rhymes are essential school tools for developing students' language and critical thinking skills. These exercises challenge students to think creatively, analyze language, and develop problem-solving strategies.*

*One of the primary benefits of riddles and rhymes is that they can improve students' language skills, including vocabulary, syntax, and grammar. By working with these exercises, students can learn new words, identify patterns in language, and develop their understanding of sentence structure and syntax.*

*Additionally, riddles and rhymes can be a fun and engaging way to learn about literary devices such as puns, metaphors, and alliteration. By analyzing these devices, students can develop a deeper appreciation for the complexity and beauty of language.*

*29. Poetry and games work on the skills of learning by doing and expressing in words—an exceptional education for school kids.*

*30. Tongue twisters and complex recitations make fun and learning possible with comics. Tongue twisters and complex recitations are often used in schools to improve student's language skills, including pronunciation, diction, and articulation. These exercises challenge students to articulate complex sounds and phrases and improve their communication ability.*

*One of the primary benefits of tongue twisters and complex recitations is that they can help students develop their speech and language skills. By practising these exercises, students can improve their ability to speak clearly and confidently, which can help them communicate effectively in various settings. Additionally, tongue twisters and complex recitations can help students develop their listening skills, as they must pay close attention to the sounds and patterns of spoken words.*

*Moreover, tongue twisters and complex recitations can be fun and engaging for learning new vocabulary and language structures. Students can use these exercises to practice new words and phrases and learn about the nuances of pronunciation and intonation in different languages. Tongue twisters and complex recitations can also help students develop their memory and concentration skills. These exercises often require students to memorize long and difficult passages, which can help them improve their ability to retain information and focus their attention for extended periods.*

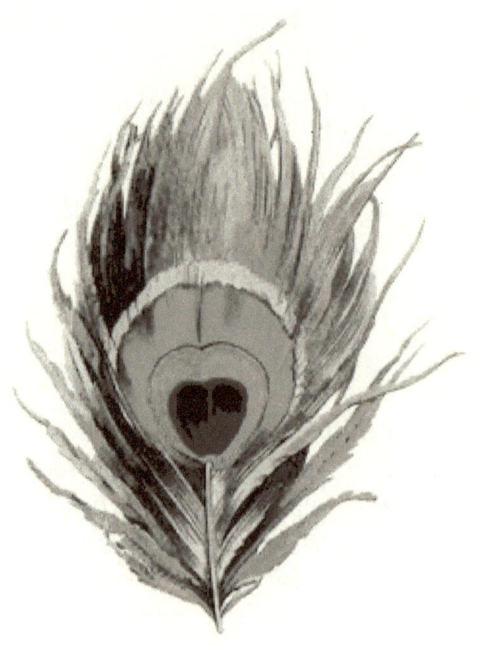

*31. Literary recitation is a priority, making learning a wow spectrum. Literary recitation by kids can have several benefits, including:*

*Improving language and communication skills: Reciting literature requires kids to use and understand complex vocabulary, grammar, and syntax. This can improve their language and communication skills, including reading, writing, and public speaking.*

*Boosting memory and concentration: Reciting literature involves memorization, which can improve memory and concentration skills in kids. Regular practice can help kids develop better recall abilities and focus.*

*Enhancing cultural awareness: Literary recitation can introduce kids to different cultures and perspectives. It can expose them to various literary genres and styles, including poetry, prose, and drama.*

*Fostering creativity and imagination: Reciting literature can stimulate kids' creativity and imagination. It can inspire them to think deeply about the meaning and themes of the work and encourage them to develop their interpretations and ideas.*

*Promoting self-confidence: Reciting literature in front of an audience can help kids develop self-confidence and self-esteem. It can allow them to showcase their talents and abilities and receive positive feedback and recognition from others.*

*32. Drama and storytelling have been of use and utility for all kids in a big way. Drama and storytelling can have numerous benefits for kids, including:*

*Enhancing creativity and imagination: Drama and storytelling allow kids to express their creativity and imagination. They can create stories, characters, and worlds and explore themes and emotions.*

*Improving language and communication skills: Engaging in drama and storytelling can help kids improve their language and communication skills. They can learn new vocabulary, grammar, and syntax and develop better reading, writing, and speaking abilities.*

*Building confidence and self-esteem: Drama and storytelling can help kids develop confidence and self-esteem. They can showcase their talents and abilities to an audience and receive positive feedback and recognition.*

*Developing social skills: Drama and storytelling can help kids develop social skills such as cooperation, collaboration, and empathy. They can work together with others to create a story or play and learn to understand and relate to different perspectives and experiences.*

*Promoting critical thinking and problem-solving: Drama and storytelling can promote critical thinking and problem-solving skills. Kids can learn to analyze and interpret stories and characters and make decisions and choices based on their understanding.*

*33. Verse composition game is a way to make the students learn about literature and even the language part of any language.*

*Verse composition games can have several benefits for kids, including:*

*Improving language skills: Verse composition games can help kids improve their language skills, including vocabulary, grammar, and syntax. It requires them to use words in creative and meaningful ways and allows them to develop a better understanding of language rules.*

*Developing creativity and imagination: Verse composition games encourage kids to use their creativity and imagination to create unique and exciting verses. This can help them develop their writing style and express themselves in new ways.*

*Enhancing critical thinking: Verse composition games require kids to think critically about the meaning and structure of the verses they compose. This can help to develop their analytical and problem-solving skills.*

*Building confidence: Engaging in verse composition games can help to build kids' confidence in their writing abilities. They can receive positive feedback from their peers and teachers and feel proud of their accomplishments.*

*Promoting teamwork and collaboration: Verse composition games can be played in groups, encouraging kids to collaborate to create a cohesive set of verses. This can help them to develop critical social skills such as communication, cooperation, and leadership.*

*34. Furniture caning, we have skills with craft and art in composition.*

*Furniture caning is weaving thin strips of rattan, wicker, or other materials through the holes of a chair or furniture frame to create a seat or backrest. While it may not seem like an activity suitable for kids, there are some benefits to teaching children this skill, including:*

*Developing fine motor skills: Furniture caning requires intricate weaving and knotting, which can help kids develop fine motor skills and hand-eye coordination.*

*Encouraging patience and persistence: Furniture caning is a time-consuming process that requires patience and perseverance. It can teach kids the value of taking their time and not giving up when faced with a challenging task.*

*Fostering creativity and problem-solving: While there are established techniques for furniture caning, there is also room for creativity and problem-solving. Kids can experiment with different patterns and materials and learn to adapt their approach to different furniture designs.*

*Building self-esteem: Completing a caning furniture project can be a source of pride and accomplishment for kids, which can help to develop their self-esteem and confidence.*

*Learning a practical skill: Furniture caning is a valuable skill kids can use throughout their lives. They can repair or restore furniture for themselves or even offer their services to others.*

*35. Sex Education as a priority for kids, as a part of SEX Education, is a priority. We teach them about SEX and childbirth. Education, on that part, is a priority and is a life skill.*

*Sex education is a crucial aspect that helps children and young adults understand their sexuality, relationships, and reproductive health. Here are some reasons why sex education is essential in schools:*

*Promotes healthy sexual behaviour: Sex education teaches young people how to make informed decisions about their sexual health, including how to protect themselves from sexually transmitted infections (STIs) and unintended pregnancies.*

*Reduces risk-taking behaviours: Sex education provides young people with the knowledge and skills to make safe and responsible decisions about their sexual behaviour, reducing the likelihood of engaging in risky behaviours such as unprotected sex.*

*Supports healthy relationships: Sex education helps young people understand healthy relationships and how to communicate effectively with their partners. It can also help them develop empathy and respect for others.*

*Addresses gender and sexuality diversity: Sex education can help young people understand and respect gender and sexuality diversity, including LGBTQ+ identities.*

*Reduces stigma and discrimination: Sex education can help reduce the stigma and discrimination associated with sexuality and reproductive health issues.*

*Improves mental health: Sex education can help young people develop positive self-esteem and body image, which can improve their mental health.*

*Helps prevent sexual abuse and assault: Sex education teaches young people about consent and boundaries, which can help prevent sexual abuse and assault.*

36. *Crafting wooden furniture is again related to the work of craftsmanship. Crafting wooden furniture is a valuable skill that can be taught in schools. It involves using specialized tools and techniques to create functional and aesthetically pleasing pieces of furniture from raw wood. This craft has practical applications in the construction industry but offers many*

benefits to students who learn it in school.

Firstly, crafting wooden furniture can help students develop their creativity and problem-solving skills. Furniture-making requires high precision, attention to detail, and critical thinking to ensure the final product is functional and meets the design specifications. Students can experiment with different designs, materials, and techniques to create unique and personalized pieces of furniture that reflect their creativity and individuality.

Secondly, woodworking can teach students essential life skills such as patience, perseverance, and focus. Creating a piece of furniture requires a lot of time and effort, and students must be patient and persistent to complete their projects successfully. This process can help students develop a strong work ethic and a sense of accomplishment as they see their projects come to fruition.

Woodworking can also teach students the value of sustainable practices and preserving natural resources. Using reclaimed or sustainably harvested wood, students can learn how to create beautiful and functional furniture while minimising environmental impact.

37. Architecture and house construction add to the architectural knowledge of science, maths and arts.

38. Distinguishing between ordinary and precious stones and metals, as a part of science and chemistry in particular.

39. Metalworking can relate to jewellery. Metalworking is an essential craft that has been around for thousands of years, and it involves shaping and forming metal into various objects using specialized tools and techniques. This craft has many practical applications, such as manufacturing tools, machines, and equipment and constructing buildings and structures.

However, metalworking also has artistic applications, where jewellery-making comes into play. Jewellery-making involves using metalworking techniques to create wearable art pieces, such as necklaces, earrings, bracelets, and rings. This craft is popular in schools, as it can be taught in art, vocational, or extracurricular activities.

The importance of metalworking in school jewellery-making lies in its several benefits to students. For one, it allows them to develop their artistic skills and creativity. Metalworking requires high precision, attention to detail, and manual dexterity, which can be challenging but rewarding.

Furthermore, metalworking can teach students essential life skills, such as patience, perseverance, problem-solving, and critical thinking. Students can also learn about the properties of different metals, how they can be manipulated to create other effects and the various techniques and tools used in metalworking.

Jewellery-making can also be a great way to explore cultural traditions and history. Many cultures have a rich history of jewellery-making, and by learning about these traditions, students can gain a greater appreciation for other cultures and broaden their worldview.

*40. Gems and mining, Teaching about gems and mining in schools can benefit students. Here are some reasons why teaching about gems and mining is important:*

*Geology education: Learning about gems and mining can provide a foundation for learning about geology. Students can learn about the different types of rocks and minerals used in mining and how they are formed. This can lead to a deeper understanding of the Earth's natural resources.*

*Economic significance: Gems and mining are important economic activities around the world. Teaching about these topics can provide students with an understanding of how the industry works, how it contributes to the global economy, and how it impacts local communities.*

*Environmental impact: Mining can have a significant effect on the environment. Teaching about the ecological impact of mining can help students understand the importance of sustainable practices and the need to protect natural resources.*

*Historical significance:* Mining has been essential from ancient times to the present. Teaching about the history of mining can help students understand the development of technology, trade, and culture over time.

*Career opportunities:* The mining industry provides many career opportunities, from geologists and engineers to equipment operators and environmental scientists. Teaching about gems and mining can help students explore potential career paths and understand the skills and education needed.

## 41. Gardening and horticulture,

*Gardening and horticulture are excellent activities for children as they provide numerous benefits to their physical, mental, and emotional well-being. Here are some reasons why gardening and horticulture are essential for kids:*

*Encourages outdoor activity: Gardening is a physical activity that enables children to enjoy fresh air and exercise.*

*Teaches responsibility: Gardening teaches children responsibility as they learn to care for and nurture plants.*

*Enhances knowledge and curiosity: Gardening and horticulture allow children to learn about plant growth, soil composition, and other aspects of nature that pique their interest.*

*Promotes healthy eating: Gardening can help promote healthy eating habits as children learn about growing and harvesting fruits and vegetables.*

*Fosters creativity: Gardening allows children to express creativity by designing and creating garden spaces.*

*Develops patience and perseverance: Gardening teaches children patience and perseverance as they wait for plants to grow and learn to problem-solve when things don't go as planned.*

*Improves mental health: Gardening and horticulture have been shown to improve mental health by reducing stress, anxiety, and depression.*

*42. Games involving animals like pets can be a fun and engaging way to teach children essential skills in schools. Here are some examples of games involving animals that can be used in the classroom:*

*Animal matching: In this game, students are given a set of cards with pictures of animals on them. They need to match the animal pictures with their corresponding names. This game helps children develop their vocabulary and memory skills.*

*Animal charades: In this game, one student acts out an animal's behaviour while the rest of the class tries to guess what animal it is. This game helps children develop their* communication and social skills.

*Pet care simulation: In this game, students take on the role of pet owners and learn how to care for their pets. This game teaches children responsibility and empathy for animals.*

*Animal trivia: In this game, students are asked questions about different animals and their habitats. This game helps children develop their knowledge of animals and the natural world.*

*Animal habitat matching: In this game, students match pictures of animals to their corresponding habitats. This game helps children develop their knowledge of animal habitats and the environment.*

*43. Training parrots and mynas to speak,*

*Teaching parrots and mynas to speak can be fun and educational for kids. Here are some of the benefits:*

*Enhances cognitive abilities: Teaching birds to speak requires patience, consistency, and repetition, which can help improve a child's cognitive abilities, including memory and problem-solving skills.*

*Promotes responsibility: Taking care of a bird and training it to speak requires accountability, which can help children learn essential life skills.*

*Foster's communication skills: Teaching birds to speak can help children develop communication skills as they learn how to interact with the bird and teach it to say.*

*Provides companionship: Birds can make excellent companions for children, and teaching them to speak can enhance the bond between the bird and the child.*

*Builds confidence: Successfully teaching a bird to speak can give children a sense of accomplishment and boost their confidence.*

*Encourages empathy: Caring for a bird and teaching it to speak can help children develop empathy and a sense of compassion for animals.*

*44. Hairdressing is not typically a priority or a part of the curriculum in most schools. However, some vocational and technical schools offer cosmetology programs, including hairdressing as one of the subjects.*

*Schools must provide a well-rounded education covering various subjects and skills, including academic subjects, physical education, arts, and vocational education. While hairdressing can be a fun and creative activity, it may not be a priority for all students and should not be the sole focus of their education.*

*Additionally, it is essential to ensure that school hairdressing programs are age-appropriate and safe for students. Safety should always be a top priority for any vocational education. Schools should ensure that they have qualified instructors and proper equipment to provide a safe learning environment for their students.*

*45. Coding messages, Coding is a valuable skill that can help students develop problem-solving, critical thinking, and creativity. Depending on age and skill level, there are several ways to introduce coding messages to school kids.*

*For younger students, visual programming languages such as Scratch or Blockly can be a great way to introduce coding concepts in a fun and interactive way. These tools allow students to drag and drop code blocks to create simple programs or animations without typing complex code.*

*For older students, text-based programming languages such as Python or JavaScript can be introduced to teach more advanced coding concepts. Students can learn how to write code to create games, websites, or other applications.*

*One fun way to introduce coding messages for kids is to create coding challenges or puzzles where students must use their coding skills to solve a problem or complete a task. These challenges can be designed to be age-appropriate and can encourage students to think creatively and experiment with different coding concepts.*

*Overall, introducing coding messages to kids in schools can be a great way to help them develop valuable skills and prepare them for a technology-driven future.*

*46. Speaking in code, Speaking in code, or using a specialized language to communicate with others, can have several benefits in schools, particularly when it comes to teaching computer programming and coding skills.*

*One of the main benefits of speaking in code is that it can help students develop critical thinking and problem-solving skills. By breaking down complex problems into smaller, more manageable parts, students can learn how to think logically and systematically, an essential skill for computer programming.*

*Additionally, speaking in code can help students communicate more effectively with each other and their teachers when discussing programming concepts and working on coding projects together. It can also help build community among students interested in programming and technology.*

*Another essential aspect of speaking in code is that it can help students develop a deeper understanding of programming concepts and syntax. By using the specialized vocabulary and syntax of a particular programming language, students can create a more intuitive sense of how the language works and how to write efficient and effective code.*

*47. Knowledge of foreign languages and dialects can be essential to a student's school education, as it can help them develop valuable skills and competencies. One of the main benefits of learning a foreign language is that it can help students develop their communication skills. Students can become more effective communicators by learning to speak and understand another language. They can also create a greater appreciation and understanding of other cultures and ways of life, promoting mutual understanding and respect.*

*48. Making flower carriages, Making flower carriages can be a fun and creative activity for students in schools, and it can also have several educational benefits. One of the main benefits of making flower carriages is that it can help students develop their artistic and creative skills. By working with flowers and other natural materials, students can learn to express themselves through art and design and build their sense of aesthetics and beauty. In addition to artistic skills, making flower carriages can help students build teamwork and collaboration skills. By working together to plan and create a flower carriage, students can learn how to communicate effectively, share ideas, and work towards a common goal.*

*Another essential benefit of making flower carriages is that they can promote environmental awareness and sustainability. Students can learn the importance of preserving and protecting the environment by using natural materials and creating something beautiful. They can develop a greater appreciation for the beauty and diversity of the natural world.*

*49. Spells, charms and omens, In educational settings, it is essential to prioritize evidence-based knowledge and critical thinking. While the cultural and historical significance of spells, treats, and warnings may be recognized and discussed in contexts such as literature, history, or anthropology classes, it is essential to avoid promoting unfounded beliefs or practices as legitimate or beneficial. Instead, modern education emphasizes the importance of critical thinking and evidence-based reasoning. This involves teaching students how to evaluate claims, assess evidence, and make informed decisions based on reliable sources of information. Moreover, promoting beliefs in spells, charms, and omens can harm students. It can lead to irrational and superstitious thinking, negatively affecting their academic and personal lives. Additionally, it can reinforce harmful stereotypes and biases that marginalise certain groups.*

*50. Making simple mechanical devices, Making simple mechanical devices can be an engaging and rewarding activity for kids in schools, and it can also have several educational benefits. One of the main benefits of making mechanical devices is that it can help students develop their problem-solving and critical-thinking skills. By designing and building robotic devices, students can learn how to identify problems, generate and evaluate possible solutions, and implement them effectively. In addition to problem-solving skills, making mechanical devices can help students develop their creativity and innovation. By experimenting with different designs and materials, students can explore new ideas and solutions and learn to think outside the box to create something unique and functional. Another essential benefit of making mechanical devices is that they can promote hands-on learning and practical skills. By working with tools and materials, students can learn how to use their hands to create something tangible and valuable and develop a range of practical skills,*

*such as measuring, cutting, drilling, and assembly.*

51. *Memory training can be essential to a student's education. It can help them improve their ability to retain and recall information,*

*which is necessary for success in academic settings.*

*One of the main benefits of memory training is that it can help students improve their working memory, which is the ability to hold and manipulate information in the short term. This can be particularly helpful for students who struggle with attention and focus, as working memory is a key component of many academic tasks, such as reading comprehension, problem-solving, and mathematical reasoning.*

*Memory training can also help students improve their long-term memory by storing and retrieving information over extended periods. This can be particularly helpful for students who need to memorize large amounts of data, such as vocabulary words, historical dates, or scientific concepts.*

*52. The game of reciting verses from hearing, also known as "Hifz al-Quran," is a valuable educational tool that can benefit school students, particularly in religious and cultural contexts.*

*One of the main benefits of this game is that it can help students develop their listening and memory skills. By listening carefully to the recitation of Quranic verses, students can learn how to recognize and recall specific verses from memory, an essential skill for religious and academic contexts.*

*Additionally, the game of reciting verses from the hearing can help students develop a deeper understanding and appreciation of the Quranic text. By memorizing and reciting specific verses, students can create a more intimate relationship with the text and gain a deeper understanding of its meaning and significance.*

*The game of reciting verses from the hearing can also help to build a sense of community and shared values among students. By engaging in this activity together, students can develop a sense of camaraderie and respect for each other's religious and cultural traditions, which can help to promote mutual understanding and respect.*

*53. Decoding messages is an essential skill for kids in schools because it helps them understand the meaning of written or spoken language. This skill is critical in reading comprehension, essential for academic success across all subjects. Here are some reasons why decoding messages is necessary for kids in schools:*

*Reading comprehension: Decoding messages is the foundation of reading comprehension. It allows students to decode and understand the meaning of words, phrases, and sentences. Students can focus on understanding the text when they can interpret words quickly and accurately.*

*Academic success: Decoding messages is a crucial skill for academic success. Students who struggle with decoding may have difficulty understanding the content in textbooks, class discussions, and other reading materials. They may also work with writing, as they may not understand how words and sentences are constructed.*

54. *Meaning of words, Understanding the meaning of words is an essential skill for school kids. It is foundational reading comprehension, critical thinking, and practical communication skill. When students encounter new words, they need to be able to use context clues, such as the surrounding words and sentences, to understand the meaning. Without this skill, students may struggle with comprehension and fall behind in their reading skills.*

55. *Dictionary studies are an essential component of language learning in schools. It helps students develop their vocabulary by*

*introducing them to new words and their meanings. Using a dictionary, students can look up unfamiliar words and learn their definitions, expanding their language knowledge. Using a dictionary can improve students' reading comprehension by helping them understand the meanings of unknown words they encounter while reading. When students can comprehend the importance of the words, they can better understand the text as a whole.*

## 56. Prosody and rhetoric,

*Prosody refers to spoken or written language's rhythm, stress, and intonation patterns. It involves the study of the sound and rhythm of speech, including pitch, volume, tempo, and duration of sounds.*

*Prosody is an essential aspect of language because it can convey emotions, attitudes, and meanings beyond the literal meaning of words. It can also create a mood or tone or emphasize certain words or phrases.*

*Rhetoric, on the other hand, is the art of persuasive communication. It involves using language to persuade or influence an audience, often through rhetorical devices such as repetition, analogy, metaphor, and rhetorical questions.*

*Rhetoric can be used in various contexts, including public speaking, writing, and advertising. It is used to create persuasive arguments and convince others to adopt a certain point of view or take a particular action.*

## 57. Impersonation,

*Impersonation means imitating or mimicking another person's behaviour, speech, or mannerisms. It can be a helpful technique in learning, as it allows individuals to model the behaviour of someone they admire or aspire to be like.*

*For example, a student who wants to become a successful public speaker may choose to impersonate the speaking style of a famous orator, such as Martin Luther King Jr. or Winston Churchill. By studying how a person speaks, gestures, and uses language, the student can learn to incorporate those techniques into their speaking style.*

*Impersonation can also be used to develop skills in other areas, such as sports, music, or art. By studying the techniques of successful athletes, musicians, or artists, individuals can learn to imitate their movements, rhythms, or styles and incorporate those techniques into their practice.*

## 58. Artful dressing,

*Artful dressing means using clothing and accessories to express oneself creatively and aesthetically. It involves using clothing as a form of self-expression and conveying one's personality, mood, and individuality.*

*Artful dressing can be seen as a reflection of one's personality and can be used to communicate one's values, interests, and beliefs to others. It can also be a way of asserting one's identity and standing out from the crowd.*

*In addition to expressing oneself creatively, artful dressing can positively impact self-confidence and self-esteem. When one feels good about their appearance and style, they are more likely to feel confident and empowered in other areas.*

*Artful dressing can also be a way of connecting with others and building relationships. Through shared interests in fashion and style, individuals can bond, form social connections, and may be inspired by each other's creative expressions.*

*59. Games of dice, Games of dice are a form of gambling that involve rolling dice and betting on the outcome. While gambling can be a fun pastime for some people, it can also have negative consequences if it becomes addictive or leads to financial difficulties.*

*Games of dice can metaphorise the risks and uncertainties we all face. Like in a game of dice, we often make decisions without knowing the exact outcome or the probabilities involved. We may have to take chances and take calculated risks to achieve our goals or pursue our passions.*

*However, it is essential to approach these risks with caution and a sense of responsibility. Just as a gambler should never bet more than they can afford to lose, we should always consider the potential consequences of our actions and decisions before taking a risk.*

*Games of dice can also teach us the importance of strategy and skill. To win a game of dice, one must understand the rules, develop a process, and make wise decisions based on the available information. Similarly, we must use our knowledge, experience, and critical thinking skills to navigate challenges and make informed decisions.*

*60. The game of 'akarsha'(a dice game played on a board),*

*The game of 'akarsha' is a traditional Indian board game that is played using dice. The game has a long history and is believed to have been played by Indian royalty as far back as the 6th century AD. While the game may not have practical applications in everyday life, the skills and lessons learned through playing it can be valuable.*

*Firstly, the game of 'akarsha' can teach players about the importance of strategy and planning. The game requires players to make decisions based on the dice rolls and the game pieces' movements and to think ahead to anticipate their opponent's moves. This can help develop critical thinking skills and make wise decisions under pressure.*

*Secondly, the game of 'akarsha' can teach players about the importance of patience and persistence. The game can be challenging and may require multiple attempts before a player can achieve their goals. This can help develop resilience and the ability to persevere in the face of difficulty.*

*Thirdly, the game of 'akarsha' can teach players about the importance of sportsmanship and fair play. The game requires players to follow the rules and treat their opponents respectfully, even in the heat of competition. This can help develop a sense of fairness and empathy towards others.*

*Finally, the game of 'akarsha' can provide a fun and engaging way to connect with others and build relationships. Playing games together can be a social and bonding experience and help develop communication and teamwork skills.*

*While the game of 'akarsha' may not have practical applications in everyday life, the skills and lessons learned through playing it can be valuable in many areas of life, including critical thinking, resilience, sportsmanship, and social connection.*

*61. Making dolls and toys for children,*

*Making dolls and toys for children can have several benefits and relevance in their development. Here are some of them:*

*Enhances creativity: Making dolls and toys can be a fun and creative activity that allows* children to express their imagination and ideas. They can create characters, stories, and worlds and explore different materials and techniques.

Promotes problem-solving skills: Creating dolls and toys can also help children develop problem-solving skills as they figure out how to construct their creations and make them work.

Develops fine motor skills: Making dolls and toys can improve children's fine motor skills as they learn to use tools like scissors, glue, and paintbrushes and manipulate materials like fabric, paper, and clay.

Foster's independence and self-esteem: Making dolls and toys can also promote independence and self-esteem as children learn to take ownership of their creations and feel proud of their accomplishments.

Encourages imaginative play: Playing with dolls and toys that children have made themselves can inspire imaginative play and help children develop social and emotional skills as they interact with their creations and others.

*Promotes sustainable and eco-friendly habits:* Making dolls and toys can encourage sustainable and eco-friendly practices as children learn to repurpose materials and reduce waste.

## 62. Personal etiquette and animal training,

*Personal etiquette and animal training are two different concepts, but both have relevance in life.*

*Personal etiquette refers to social conventions and behaviours considered appropriate and polite in different situations, such as in public, work, or social gatherings. Personal etiquette involves using good manners, respecting others, and displaying appropriate behaviour.*

*Relevance in life:*

*Builds positive relationships: Personal etiquette can help build positive relationships with others. When we display good manners and respectful behaviour, it can make others feel valued and appreciated.*

*Improves communication: Personal etiquette can enhance communication by promoting active listening, clear communication, and understanding.*

*Promotes professionalism: Personal etiquette is essential in professional settings, such as the workplace or business meetings. Good manners and professional behaviour can help build a positive reputation and career advancement opportunities.*

*On the other hand, animal training refers to teaching animals specific behaviours or responses through positive reinforcement, negative reinforcement, or punishment. Animal activity can teach pets basic obedience, help animals perform particular tasks, or even be used in wildlife conservation efforts.*

*Relevance in life:*

*Helps establish a bond with animals: Animal training can help establish a bond between humans and animals, particularly pets. This bond can be beneficial for both the animal and the human.*

*Enhances safety: Animal training can improve security by teaching animals to appropriate behaviour and responses. For example, training dogs to obey commands like 'stay' or 'come' can prevent accidents or injuries.*

*Encourages problem-solving skills: Animal training can also promote problem-solving skills in animals and humans. Determining the best way to teach a particular behaviour can require creativity, critical thinking, and patience.*

*In conclusion, personal etiquette and animal training are two different concepts, but both have relevance in life. Personal etiquette can help build positive relationships, improve communication, and promote professionalism. Animal training can help establish a bond with animals, enhance safety, and encourage problem-solving skills.*

*63. Knowledge of dharmic warfare and victory,*

*In the context of Indian philosophy and culture, the knowledge of dharmic warfare and victory has relevance in several ways:*

*Understanding dharma: Dharmic warfare involves fighting for a just cause and upholding dharma or righteousness. Therefore, the knowledge of dharmic warfare helps people understand the concept of dharma and the importance of living a righteous life.*

*Developing moral and ethical values: The principles of dharmic warfare emphasize the importance of honesty, integrity, and righteousness in all aspects of life. Thus, the knowledge of dharmic warfare can help individuals develop strong moral and ethical values.*

*Cultivating courage and discipline: Dharmic warfare requires immense courage, discipline, and sacrifice. Understanding the principles of dharmic warfare can help individuals cultivate these virtues and develop the mental and physical strength to face difficult situations in life.*

*Promoting peace and harmony: Despite being a form of warfare, the principles of dharmic action emphasize the importance of peace and harmony. Therefore, the knowledge of dharmic action can help individuals understand the value of peaceful coexistence and work towards promoting harmony in society.*

*Achieving victory in life: Victory in dharmic warfare is about defeating one's enemies and attaining inner peace and contentment. Therefore, the knowledge of dharmic action can help individuals achieve victory by cultivating a sense of purpose, discipline, and righteousness.*

*In conclusion, the knowledge of dharmic warfare and victory has relevance in developing moral and ethical values, cultivating courage and discipline, promoting peace and harmony, and achieving success in life.*

*64. Physical culture. Physical culture, which refers to the cultivation of physical fitness and well-being through exercise, sports, and other physical activities, has great relevance in human lives for several reasons:*

*Promotes physical health: Regular physical activities can help maintain physical health by improving cardiovascular health, muscle strength, and flexibility. Physical fitness can also help prevent chronic health conditions such as obesity, diabetes, and heart disease.*

*Improves mental health: Exercise and physical activity have been shown to positively affect mental health, reducing symptoms of depression and anxiety and improving mood and self-esteem.*

*Enhances cognitive function: Physical activity has also been shown to improve cognitive function, including memory, attention, and decision-making skills.*

*Foster's social connections: Physical activities and sports can provide opportunities for social interaction and connection, improving mental health and overall well-being.*

*Enhances quality of life: Physical fitness can help individuals enjoy a better quality of life by improving their overall health, mental health, and social connections.*

*Increases longevity: Regular physical activity has been associated with increased longevity, as it helps prevent chronic health conditions and promotes overall health and well-being.*

*In conclusion, physical culture is essential in human lives because it promotes physical health, improves mental health and cognitive function, fosters social connections, enhances the quality of life, and increases longevity. Incorporating physical activities into one's daily routine can benefit overall health and well-being.*

# CHAPTER TWO

# IMPORTANCE OF 64 KALAS

*According to Hindu mythology, Lord Krishna
is believed to embody all the arts and skills in*

the world. In Hindu mythology and culture, the 64 Kalas of Lord Krishna are held in very high esteem and are thought to be of tremendous significance. These arts and skills are revered as a source of inspiration and guidance for anyone seeking to improve their skills and enrich their lives through creative expression. They are believed to embody the highest form of knowledge and are revered as the embodiment of this most elevated form of learning.

The 64 Kalas reflect Lord Krishna's mastery of these skills and his conviction in the significance of artistic and creative expression. This belief is reflected in the 64 Kalas. They often represent a holistic approach to education, which considers practical skills and moral and ethical considerations. Since they are seen to be able to nurture inner and exterior harmony, the arts are also a good reminder of how important it is to strike a healthy balance in one's life.

In addition to their aesthetic value, the 64 Kalas are also seen as having potential uses in the real world. They are thought to be beneficial not only for one's personal growth and development but also for establishing and maintaining good connections with other people. For instance, the art of dialogue, also known as Samvada, is an essential instrument *for precise and efficient communication. In contrast, the art of sports, also known as Kalakrida, is thought to improve physical health and mental agility.*

*The 64 Kalas of Lord Krishna, taken as a whole, are an essential component of Indian culture and stand for a varied and illustrious tradition of aesthetic and creative expression. They serve as a helpful reminder of the significance of obtaining a diverse education and the importance of creative expression in enhancing our lives and fostering personal growth and development.*

*The 64 Kalas, also known as the 64 arts, are said to be the various artistic and creative skills that Lord Krishna possessed and exhibited throughout his life. These 64 Kalas are considered the highest form of knowledge and are revered by many in the Hindu culture.*

*Some of the 64 Kalas of Lord Krishna include:*

*Nritya - The art of dance*

*Sangeet - The art of music*

*Vastu - The art of architecture*

*Chitrakala - The art of painting*

*Kavya - The art of poetry*

*Hasta Mudras - The art of hand gestures*

*Shilp - The art of sculpture*

*Samvada - The art of conversation*

*Vina Vadana - The art of playing musical instruments*

*Kalakrida - The art of sports*

*These 64 Kalas are considered an integral part of Indian culture and are often taught in traditional schools of arts and crafts. Many people continue to practice and master these arts today, as they are believed to have immense spiritual and aesthetic value.*

*In Hinduism, Lord Krishna is revered as the ultimate guide and teacher, and the 64 Kalas are considered to be an embodiment of his teachings. They are also believed to be a source of inspiration and guidance for anyone seeking to improve their skills and enrich their lives through creative expression.*

# CHAPTER THREE

# IMPORTANCE OF PEACOCK FEATHER

*In Hindu mythology, Krishna is sometimes pictured with a peacock feather tucked into his mane. The peacock feather is essential and may be interpreted in several ways. The importance of the peacock feather to Lord Krishna may be broken down into many categories, including*

*the following:*

*The peacock is a bird well-known for its beauty and elegance, and its feather is often regarded as among the most beautiful in the world. Peacocks are thought to be a symbol of beauty and grace. Lord Krishna wears the peacock feather to represent his beauty and elegance. Lord Krishna is often connected with love and attractiveness.*

*It is stated that the peacock feather represents Lord Krishna's triumph over negativity and evil. The peacock is renowned for its capacity to ingest venomous snakes, and its feather symbolises this victory.*

*Peacock feathers are considered to signify enlightenment and spiritual achievement, and some people believe that they also reflect spiritual accomplishment. Culture on a spiritual level is symbolized here by Lord Krishna, who is believed to be an incarnation of Lord Vishnu. This is the pinnacle of one's spiritual journey.*

*The peacock feather is regarded as a talisman of protection in certain cultures, believing it has the power to ward off evil energies. The peacock feather symbolises the protection that Lord Krishna, guardian of his followers, wears on his head.*

*It is stated that the love and devotion of Lord Krishna's devotees is represented by the peacock feather, which is widely connected with heavenly love because of Lord Krishna's frequent association with it.*

*In a nutshell, the peacock feather is a significant emblem in Hindu mythology. It is connected to concepts such as divine love, divine beauty, the triumph of good over evil, spiritual advancement, divine protection, and victory over adversity. The peacock feather that Lord Krishna wore was symbolic of many things, including his beauty and elegance, his triumph over negativity, his protection of his devotees, and his portrayal of the ultimate aim of achieving spiritual enlightenment.*

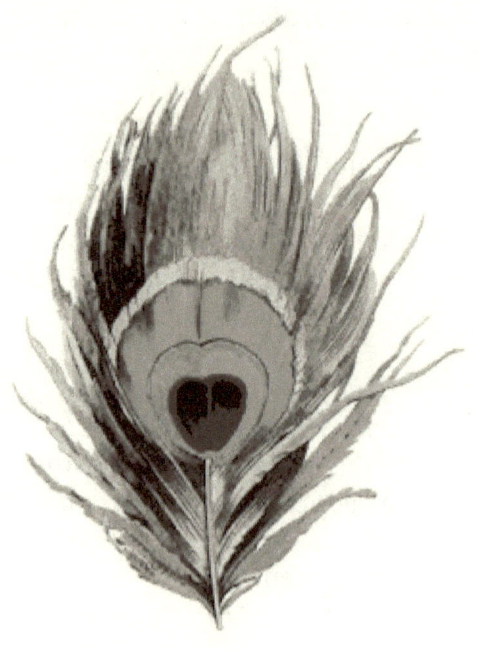

# CHAPTER FOUR

# REFERENCES

https://rkmvcc.org/mala-grathana-kids

https://invajy.com/
8-life-changing-lessons-to-learn-from-lord-krishna/

https://ritikalalwani.medium.com/
use-lord-krishnas-teachings-for-better-decision-
making-25eb662d5e0e

https://www.amritapuri.org/3605/sri-krishna.aum

https://www.srinannagaru.com/books/
LordKrishnaTheDecoratedGod.pdf

https://www.speakingtree.in/allslides/
15-amazing-teaching-of-lord-krishna

https://www.stephen-knapp.com/
lord_krishna_and_his_essential_teachings.htm

# About The Author

Dheeraj Mehrotra, MS, MPhil, PhD (Education Management) honoris causa., a white and a yellow belt in SIX SIGMA, a Certified NLP Business Diploma holder, is an Educational Innovator, Author, with expertise in Six Sigma In Education, Academic Audits, Neuro-Linguistic Programming (NLP), Total Quality Management In Education, an Experiential Educator, a CBSE Resource towards School Assessment (SQAA), CCE, JIT, Five S and KAIZEN. He has authored over 40 books on Computer Science for ICSE/ ISC/ CBSE Students, over 50 books of academic interest for education excellence and Six Sigma.

A former Principal at De Indian Public School, New Delhi (INDIA), with an ample teaching experience of over Two Decades, he is a certified Trainer for Quality Circles/ TQM in Education and QCI Standards for School Accreditation/ Six Sigma in Education. He has also been honoured with the President of India's National Teacher Award in the year 2006 and the Best Science Teacher State Award (By the Ministry of Science and Technology, State of UP), Innovation in Education for his inception of Six Sigma In Education by Education Watch, New Delhi and Education World- Best Teacher Award, BOLT Learner Teacher Award by Air India, 'Innovation in Education Award 2016' by Higher Education Forum (HEF), Gujarat Chapter, among others. He has developed over 150 FREE EDUCATIONAL MOBILE Apps for the Google Play Store exclusively for Teachers, Students and Parents. This work has been recognized by the LIMCA BOOK OF RECORDS & INDIA BOOK OF RECORDS as the only Indian to draw that feast. As a premier UDEMY Instructor, he has developed over 450 Courses on UDEMY. Dr Mehrotra is a PRINCIPAL at Kunwar's Global School, Lucknow, India. He has conducted over 1000 workshops globally on "Excellence In Education" integrated with Total Quality Management and Six Sigma, Technology Integration in Education (TIE), Developing towards being ROCKSTAR TEACHERS, including Cyberspace, Cyber Security, Classroom Management, School Leadership & Management, and Innovative teaching within classrooms via Mind Maps, NLP and Experiential Learning in Academics. He is an active TEDx speaker and can be viewed on the youtube TEDx channel. He can be visited at www.authordheerajmehrotra.com

# Books By The Same Author

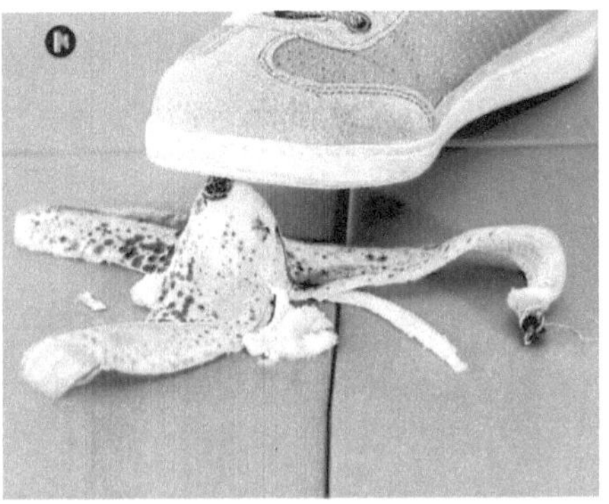

BY NATIONAL
AWARDEE
EDUCATOR
BASICS OF
ARTIFICIAL
INTELLIGENCE
&
MACHINE
LEARNING
DR. DHEERAJ MEHROTRA
authordheerajmehrotra.com
Flipkart
available at
amazon
Digital List Price: ₹ 103.95
Kindle Price: ₹ 99.00
Save ₹ 4.95 (4%)
inclusive of all taxes

BY NATIONAL
AWARDEE
EDUCATOR
Kindle Price: ₹ 72.00
inclusive of all taxes
Teaching
in the
VUCA
WORLD
Dr. Dheeraj Mehrotra
authordheerajmehrotra.com
Flipkart
available at
amazon

101
SCHOOL
MANAGEMENT
STRATEGIES
Towards EFFECTIVE
QUALITY MANAGEMENT
System in Schools
DR. DHEERAJ
MEHROTRA
Digital List Price: ₹72.45
M.R.P.: ₹199.00
Kindle Price: ₹ 69.00
Save ₹ 130.00 (65%)
inclusive of all taxes
amazon
www.authordheerajmehrotra.com

FOR
QUALITY
TEACHING
Maximizing
Learning
Potential of Kids
TOWARDS EXCELLENCE IN
TEACHING & LEARNING
200
WOW TEACHING
IDEAS
DR. DHEERAJ MEHROTRA
amazon
₹270.00
M.R.P.: ₹300.00
www.authordheerajmehrotra.com

*"The true aim of education is to awaken the child's curiosity and creativity, to encourage their natural inclination towards learning, and to cultivate their character and values so that they become not only knowledgeable but also wise and compassionate human beings." ...... Lord Krishna*